Better Drums With.

Rockschool

A *Rockschool* Publication
245 Sandycombe Road, Kew, Richmond, Surrey, TW9 2EW

14.99
no VAT

Welcome To *Drums* Grade 2

Welcome to the Rockschool *Drums* Grade 2 pack. The book and CD contain everything needed to play drums in this grade. The CD has full stereo mixes of each tune and backing tracks to play along with for practice. Handy tips on playing the pieces and the marking schemes can be found in the Guru's Guide on page 15. If you have any queries about this or any other Rockschool exam, please call us on **020 8332 6303** or email us at office@rockschool.co.uk or visit our website http://www.rockschool.co.uk. Good luck!

Player Zone Techniques in Grade 2 and Grade 3

The eight Rockschool grades are divided into four Zones. *Drums* Grade 2, along with Grade 3, is part of the *Player Zone*. This Zone is for those of you who are building on key skills to express your musical personality across a range of styles.

Grade 2: in this grade you use a range of physical and expressive techniques with confidence, including effective left and right hand co-ordination, effective use of both feet to play combinations of any two voices together, as well as the use of double sticking. You are also beginning to use a range of dynamics from quiet (*p*) to loud (*f*). It is in this grade that you are starting to develop your ability to play with stylistic authority.

Grade 3: as a player you will be confident in a range of physical and expressive techniques, including the use of the toe and heel for hi hat and kick drum playing, and tasteful use of cymbals. You will be broadening your dynamic range and be able to demonstrate your abilities across a number of styles.

Drums Grade 2 Exam

Players wishing to enter for a *Drums* Grade 2 exam need to prepare **three** pieces, of which **one** may be a free choice piece chosen from outside the printed repertoire. In addition, you must prepare the technical exercises in this book, undertake either a sight reading test or an improvisation & interpretation test, take an ear test and answer general musicianship questions. Samples of these are printed in the book.

Further information on the *Drums* Grade 2 exam can be found in the Guru's Guide on page 15.

Drum Notation Explained

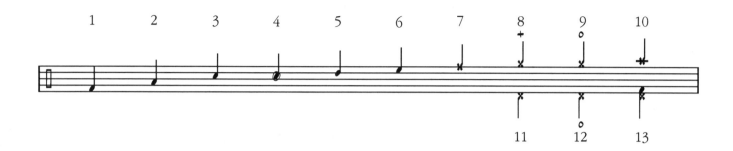

1. Kick drum
2. Floor tom
3. Snare drum
4. Rim shot
5. Medium tom
6. High tom
7. Ride cymbal
8. Hi hat closed
9. Hi hat open
10. Crash cymbal
11. Hi hat (foot)
12. Hi hat open (foot)
13. Hi hat & kick drum together

General Musical Notation

Accent: Accentuate note (play it louder)

Accent: Accentuate note with great intensity

Repeat Bars: Repeat the bars between the repeat indications.

1st and 2nd Time Repeat Endings: When a repeated section has different endings, play the 1st ending only the 1st time, and the 2nd ending only the second time.

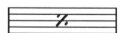

1 Bar Repeat: Repeat previous bar. In higher grades these may also be marked *sim.*

2 Bar Repeat: Repeat the previous 2 bars. In higher grades these may also be marked *sim.*

D.C. AL FINE

Da Capo Al Fine: Go back to the beginning of the song and play until the bar marked FINE (end).

D.S. AL CODA

Dal Segno Al Coda: Go back to the sign (𝄋), then play until the bar marked TO CODA ⊕ then skip to the section marked ⊕ CODA.

One Star

Song 2

Nic France

♩=90 BRIT POP

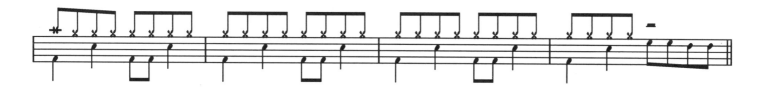

Don't Ever Stop

Adrian York

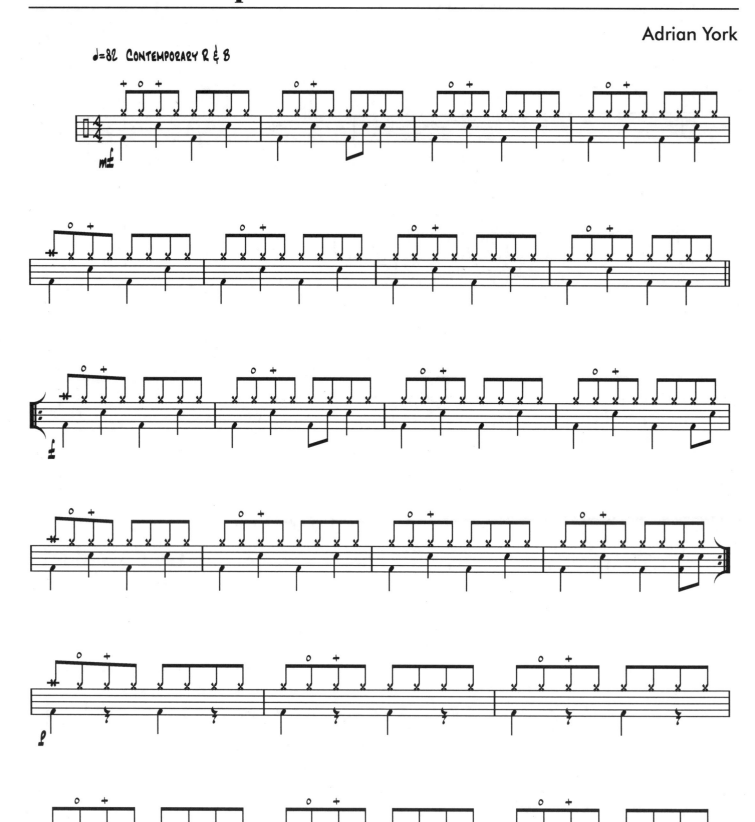

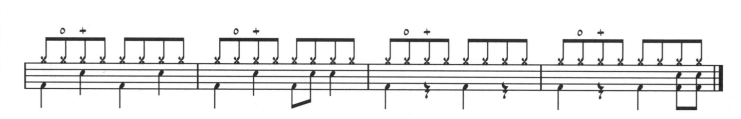

Freetime

Hussein Boon

Tidy

Calum Rees

Drums Grade 2

Hitsville

Adrian York

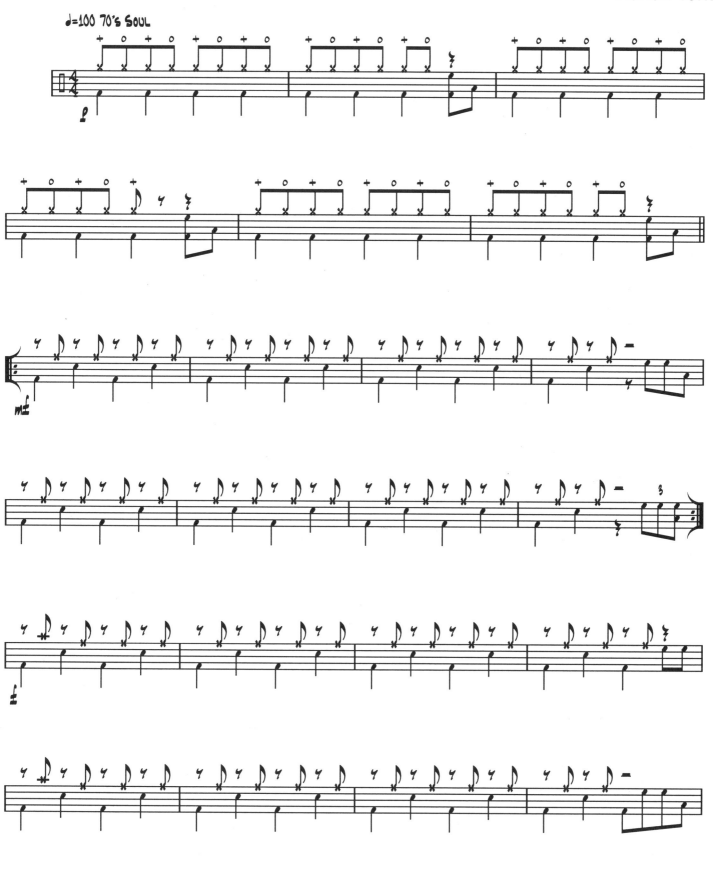

Technical Exercises

In this section, the examiner will ask you to play a selection of exercises drawn from each of the five groups shown below. You do not need to memorise the exercises (and can use the book in the exam) but the examiner will be looking for the speed of your response. The examiner will also give credit for the level of your musicality.

The ⌐ and ⌐ markings shown underneath the notes represent the sticking patterns: leading hand and following hand.

Group A: Single strokes   ♩ = 70

a) In 8th notes

b) In triplet 8th notes

Group B: Double strokes   ♩ = 70

a) In 8th notes

Group C: Paradiddles   ♩ = 70

a) Standard paradiddle in 16th notes

b) Inverted paradiddle in 16th notes

Entering an Exam

Please use one, or a combination, of these forms to enter the exam(s) of your choice. Fill out the details as requested below and send the form, along with the appropriate fees, to:

Exam Entries, Rockschool, 245 Sandycombe Road, Kew, Richmond, Surrey, TW9 2EW

There are three examination periods per year for which you may enter. The closing dates for these are shown in the table below.

PERIOD	DURATION	CLOSING DATE
Period A	1st February to 15th March	1st December
Period B	15th May to 31st July	1st April
Period C	1st November to 15th December	1st October

You can get up to date information on examination prices by ringing the Rockschool help line on **020 8332 6303** Please make cheques or postal orders payable to **Rock School Ltd**.

Grade Exam Entry Form

Full Name								
Address								
Post Code								
Telephone								
Instrument	Guitar ☐		Bass ☐			Drums ☐		
Grade	Debut ☐	1 ☐	2 ☐	3 ☐	4 ☐	5 ☐	6 ☐	8 ☐
Period	A ☐		B ☐		C ☐			
Year								
Fee								
Please state any dates that are absolutely impossible for you to attend								

ROCKSCHOOL HELPLINE: 020 8332 6303
email: office@rockschool.co.uk   internet: www.rockschool.co.uk

The International Examinations Board

i

Performance Certificate Exam Entry Form

You can enter for one of three Performance Certificates using the Rockschool materials:

- *Player Zone*, using the Grade 3 repertoire pieces
- *Performer Zone*, using the Grade 5 repertoire pieces
- *Pro Zone*, using the Grade 8 repertoire pieces

To enter for one (or more) of these exams, please fill in your details as requested below and send the form, along with the appropriate fees, to:

Exam Entries, Rockschool, 245 Sandycombe Road, Kew, Richmond, Surrey, TW9 2EW

You can get up to date information on examination prices by ringing the Rockschool help line on **020 8332 6303** Please make cheques or postal orders payable to **Rock School Ltd**.

Full Name					
Address					
Post Code					
Telephone					
Instrument	Guitar ☐		Bass ☐	Drums	☐
Zone	Player ☐	Performer ☐		Pro	☐
Period	A ☐	B ☐	C	☐	
Year					
Fee					
Please state any dates that are absolutely impossible for you to attend					

ROCKSCHOOL HELPLINE: 020 8332 6303
email: office@rockschool.co.uk   internet: www.rockschool.co.uk

Band Exam Entry Form

You can enter as a band (1 guitar player, 1 bass player and 1 drummer) for one of three Band Exams using the Rockschool materials:

- *Player Zone*, using the Grade 3 repertoire pieces
- *Performer Zone*, using the Grade 5 repertoire pieces
- *Pro Zone*, using the Grade 8 repertoire pieces

To enter for one (or more) of these exams, please fill in your details as requested below and send the form, along with the appropriate fees, to:

Exam Entries, Rockschool, 245 Sandycombe Road, Kew, Richmond, Surrey, TW9 2EW

You can get up to date information on examination prices by ringing the Rockschool help line on **020 8332 6303** Please make cheques or postal orders payable to **Rock School Ltd**.

Band Contact Name	
Address	
	Post Code
Telephone	

Player's Name	Instrument	Zone	Fee
		Total fees enclosed	£

Period	A ☐	B ☐	C ☐
Year			
Please state any dates that are absolutely impossible for you to attend			

The International Examinations Board

Teacher's Exam Entry Form

Teachers wishing to enter grade exams and performance certificates on behalf of their students should complete the form and send it, along with the appropriate fees, to

Exam Entries, Rockschool, 245 Sandycombe Road, Kew, Richmond, Surrey, TW9 2EW
(All band exam entries should be on the band exam entry form.)

You can get up to date information on examination prices by ringing the Rockschool help line on **020 8332 6303** Please make cheques or postal orders payable to **Rock School Ltd**.

Teacher's Name	
Address	
	Post Code
Telephone	

Player's Name	Instrument	Grade	Perf.Cert.	Period	Year	Fee
					Total fees enclosed	£

Please state any dates that are absolutely impossible for you to attend

ROCKSCHOOL HELPLINE: 020 8332 6303
email: office@rockschool.co.uk   internet: www.rockschool.co.uk

The International Examinations Board

Group D: Flams   ♩ = 70

a) Flams in quarter notes

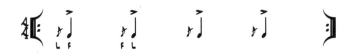

Group E: Triplets   ♩ = 70

a) Standard triplet in 8th notes

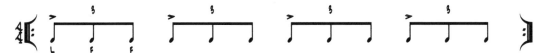

Sight Reading *or* Improvisation & Interpretation

In this section you have a choice between either a sight reading test or an improvisation & interpretation test. Printed below is an example of the type of **sight reading** test you are likely to encounter in the exam. The examiner will allow you 90 seconds to prepare it and will set the tempo for you on a metronome.

Printed below is an example of the type of **improvisation & interpretation** test you are likely to encounter in an exam. You will be asked to play an improvised groove for 8 bars in one of the following styles: blues, rock, funk or jazz. The basis of the groove to be improvised is given in the first two bars. The examiner will allow you 90 seconds to prepare it and will set the tempo for you on a metronome.

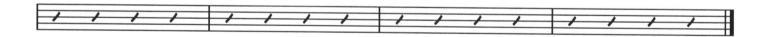

Ear Tests

You will find two ear tests in this grade. The examiner will play each test to you twice on CD.

Test 1

You will be asked to identify a drum fill made up of a number of note value combinations played on the snare drum. An example of this type of test is shown below.

Answer: (i) a pair of 8th notes
(ii) a quarter note
(iii) a pair of 8th notes
(iv) two 16th notes and an 8th note

Test 2

You will be asked to play back on your drums a four bar drum groove using the following drum voices: crash cymbal, hi hat, snare drum and kick drum. An example of this type of test is shown below.

General Musicianship Questions

You will be asked five General Musicianship Questions at the end of the exam.

Topics:

i)   Musical knowledge
ii) Knowledge of your instrument

The musical knowledge questions will cover the following topics at this grade:

Recognition of drum voices on the stave
Note values
Rests
Time signatures
Dynamic markings (*p*, *mp*, *mf* and *f*)
Repeat markings (including first and second time bars)
Cresc. and *dim.*

The instrument knowledge questions will cover the following topics at this grade:

Names and position of all drum voices
Procedures for tuning drums

Questions on all these topics will be based on pieces played by you in the exam

The Guru's Guide to *Drums* Grade 2

This section contains some handy hints compiled by Rockschool's Drums Guru to help you get the most out of the performance pieces. Do feel free to adapt the tunes to suit your playing style. Remember, these tunes are your chance to show your musical imagination and personality.

Care has been taken to match the printed parts to the audio performances. Where discrepancies occur, players may either follow the printed part or devise grooves and fills to suit the style as required. Please also note the solos featured in the full mixes are not meant to be indicative of the standard required for the grade.

Drums Grade 2 Tunes

Rockschool tunes help you play the hit tunes you enjoy. The pieces have been written by top pop and rock composers and players according to style specifications drawn up by Rockschool.

The tunes printed here are divided into two groups of three pieces. The first group of pieces belongs to the *contemporary mainstream* and features current styles in today's charts. The second group of pieces consists of *roots styles*, those classic grooves and genres which influence every generation of performers.

CD full mix track 1, backing track 7: *One Star*

Modern guitar pop in the style of Ocean Colour Scene. This is a snare-kick-toms extravaganza requiring both hand and kick drum foot co-ordination and independence. This is quite fast at 110 bpm, but don't push the beat too much and watch for the rests throughout, and the triplets in bar 16.

Composer: Peter Huntington. Peter is a young drummer of some distinction with a varied session career to date, including a long stint with Mark Owen of Take That, and an appearance in Dario G's 1998 World Cup song.

CD full mix track 2, backing track 8: *Song 2*

This is a fairly straightforward Brit Pop type tune featuring standard snare and kick drum patterns along with hi hat eighths, switching to a ride pattern after bar 17. There are a couple of fills marked at the end of eight bar sections. Remember to keep the timing of these even.

Composer: Nic France. Nic is a versatile session drummer who has played with a variety of acts including Howard Jones, Working Week, Tanita Tikaram and Pete Townsend.

CD full mix track 3, backing tack 9: *Don't Ever Stop*

Contemporary R & B in the style of Eternal or R Kelly. This features a very straightforward pattern with the kick drum and snare drum played in quarter notes and the hi hat played in eighths. The opening and closing of the hi hat falls on the same beat each time it occurs.

Composer: Adrian York. Adrian has played with many famous artists such as Sandie Shaw, Jimmy Ruffin, Paul Young and Lily Savage, and is the author of the *Style File* series.

CD full mix track 4, backing track 10: *Freetime*

A 12 bar blues similar in style to 70's Clapton (check out his album *461 Ocean Boulevard*). This features a standard rock pattern with hi hat eighths for the first half before moving to ride cymbal eighths in the second half.

Composer: Hussein Boon. Hussein specialises in 'noisy pop' with a bit of drum 'n' bass thrown in. He has graced bands such as Beats International, Microgroove and De La Soul as well as artists such as Omar and Karen Ramirez.

CD full mix track 5, backing track 11: *Tidy*

Eighties rock reminiscent of Robert Palmer's *Addicted To Love*. The drum part for the first eight bars marks out the pulse before kicking in with a rock groove after bar 9 in which the hi hat is played using quarter notes. There are climactic tom-snare-kick sections in bars 15-16, and 23-24 during which you should build the intensity of the volume.

Composer: Calum Rees. Calum is a young drummer with a growing reputation. He has a number of session credits to his name and played on the Dario G 1998 World Cup song.

CD full mix track 6, backing track 12: *Hitsville*

70's soul in the style of the Jackson 5. The first eight bars feature a four to the floor kick drum pattern and akternating open and closed hi hat. This is followed by a simple quarter note kick and snare drum pattern with off beat eighth note ride cymbals.

Composer: Adrian York.

CD Musicians:

> **Guitars:** Deirdre Cartwright **Drums:** Geoff Gascoyne **Drums:** Steve Creese
> **Keyboards and programming:** Adrian York

Grade Exam Marking Scheme

The table below shows the marking scheme for the *Drums* Grade 2 exam.

ELEMENT	PASS	MERIT	DISTINCTION
Piece 1 Piece 2 Piece 3	13 out of 20 13 out of 20 13 out of 20	15 out of 20 15 out of 20 15 out of 20	17+ out of 20 17+ out of 20 17+ out of 20
Technical Exercises	11 out of 15	12 out of 15	13+ out of 15
Either: Sight Reading *Or:* Improvisation & Interpretation	6 out of 10	7 out of 10	8+ out of 10
Ear Tests	6 out of 10	7 out of 10	8+ out of 10
General Musicianship Questions	3 out of 5	4 out of 5	5 out of 5
Total Marks	**Pass: 65% +**	**Pass: 75% +**	**Pass: 85% +**

Free Choice Song Criteria

You can bring in your own performance pieces to play in any of the exams featured. In the Grade Exams you can bring in **one** piece.

You should read the following criteria carefully.

- Players may bring in either their own compositions or songs already in the public domain, including hits from the charts.

- Songs may be performed either solo or to a CD or tape backing track.

- Players should bring two paper copies of the piece to be performed. The examiner will retain one copy, which may be hand written.

- Players may perform either complete songs or extracts: such as a solo part.

- Players should aim to keep their free choice songs below 2 minutes in length.

- Players should aim to make each free choice song of a technical standard similar to those published in the Rockschool *Drums* Grade 2 book. However, examiners will be awarding credit for how well you perform the song. In general players should aim to play songs that mix the following physical and expressive techniques and rhythm skills:

Physical Techniques: accurate and independent hand and foot co-ordination.

Expressive Techniques: use of accented notes within phrases, a dynamic range (soft to loud) and simple fills.

Rhythm Skills: songs should contain a mixture of whole, half, quarter and eighth notes, dotted half and quarter notes and triplets, along with their associated rests. Songs may contain simple syncopation and be in 4/4 time signatures.

You, or your teacher, may wish to adapt an existing piece of music to suit the criteria above. You should ensure that any changes to the music are clearly marked on the sheet submitted to the examiner.

Entering Rockschool Exams

Entering a Rockschool exam is easy. Please read through these instructions carefully before filling in the exam entry form. Information on current exam fees can be obtained from Rock School by ringing **020 8332 6303**

- You should enter for a *Drums* Grade 2 exam when you feel ready.

- You can enter for any one of three examination periods. These are shown below with their closing dates.

PERIOD	DURATION	CLOSING DATE
Period A	1st February to 15th March	1st December
Period B	15th May to 31st July	1st April
Period C	1st November to 15th December	1st October

These dates will apply from 1st January 1999 until further notice

- Please fill in the form giving your name, address and phone number. Please tick the type and level of exam, along with the period and year. Finally, fill in the fee box with the appropriate amount. You should send this form with a cheque or postal order to: **Rockschool, 245 Sandycombe Road, Kew, Richmond, Surrey, TW9 2EW**

- When you enter an exam you will receive from Rockschool an acknowledgement letter containing your exam entry number along with a copy of our exam regulations.

- Rockschool will allocate your entry to a centre and you will receive notification of the exam, showing a date, location and time as well as advice of what to bring to the centre.

- You should inform Rockschool of any cancellations or alterations to the schedule as soon as you can as it is usually not possible to transfer entries from one centre, or one period, to another without the payment of an additional fee.

- Please bring your music book and CD to the exam. You may not use photocopied music, nor the music used by someone else in another exam. The examiner will stamp each book after each session. You may be barred from taking an exam if you use someone else's music.

- You should aim to arrive for your *Drums* Grade 2 exam fifteen minutes before the time stated on the schedule.

- The exam centre will have a waiting area and warm-up facilities which you may use prior to being called into the main exam room.

- Each *Drums* Grade 2 exam is scheduled to last for 20 minutes. You can use a small proportion of this time to warm up and get ready.

- About 2 to 3 weeks after the exam you will receive a typed copy of the examiner's mark sheet. Every successful player will receive a Rockschool certificate of achievement.

Exclusive Distributors:
Music Sales Ltd
Newmarket Road, Bury St Edmunds
Suffolk IP33 3YB

Published by Rock School Ltd © 1999

Compiled and Edited by Simon Pitt, Simon Troup & Norton York
Editorial Assistants: Hussein Boon & Peter Huntington
Syllabus manager: Adrian York
Syllabus consultants: Deirdre Cartwright, Geoff Gascoyne and Paul Cameron
Audio producer: Adrian York
Audio engineer: Alan Fisher

Music processing: Simon Troup and Jenny Harrison of Digital Music Art
Cover Design: Bet Ayer

Printed in the United Kingdom by
Caligraving Ltd, Thetford, England

Your Guarantee of Quality
As publishers we strive to produce every book to the highest commercial standards.
The music has been freshly engraved and the book has been carefully designed to minimise
awkward page turns and to make playing from it a real pleasure. Particular care has been
given to specifying acid free, neutral-sized paper made from pulps which have not
been elemental chlorine bleached. This pulp is from farmed sustainable forests,
and produced with special regard for the environment. Throughout, the printing and
binding have been planned to ensure a sturdy, attractive publication which
should give you years of enjoyment. If your copy fails to meet our high standards,
please inform us and we will gladly replace it.

Visit the Rockschool Website at
www.rockschool.co.uk

The full Rockschool publication list can be obtained from
245 Sandycombe Road
Kew, Richmond, Surrey TW9 2EW

Phone 020 8332 6303
Fax 020 8332 6297

DRUMS

rock school

➤ **Rockschool** is about playing the styles of music you enjoy. Our specially written tunes develop the key skills, styles and techniques you need so you can play the hits of today, yesterday and tomorrow.

➤ The **Rockschool** packs have standard music notation plus great sounding CDs featuring top musicians. We also encourage everyone to be creative with our **Rockschool** tunes – so feel free to improvise and adapt them to suit your playing style and musical approach.

➤ This pack contains the tunes from **Grade 2** in the **Player Zone**. This is for those of you who are building on key skills to express your musical personality across a range of styles. To help you progress quickly, read our 'Guru's Guide' where you will find hints on playing each tune. There is also a description of all the playing achievements you need to aim for in the **Player Zone**, both for **Grade 2** and **Grade 3**, so you can have an overview of your progress at a glance.

➤ Our **Rockschool** grades are accredited by **Trinity College London**. When you take one of our **Rockschool** exams you will have a qualification and measure of your achievement that is recognised around the world. It shows that you can play your music when it really counts.

We know you will achieve great results from playing **Drums** with **Rockschool**. Enjoy!

rock school

245 Sandycombe Road
Kew, Richmond,
Surrey TW9 2EW
Tel:020 8332 6303
email: office@rockschool.co.uk
internet: www.rockschool.co.uk

Trinity
The International Examinations Board

catalogue no. RSK 019919

ISBN 1-902775-18-X

9 781902 775180